76712

Hailstones and Halibut Bones

ADVENTURES IN COLOR

Hailstones and Halibut Bones

By

MARY O'NEILL

newly illustrated by

JOHN WALLNER

DOUBLEDAY

NEW YORK LONDON TORONTO SYDNEY AUCKLAND

This book is lovingly dedicated to my children and grandchildren
and to all those who see and feel the wonders of color
either with sight or through their imagination.
M.O.

For Diana Klemin
with many thanks
J.C.W.

Published by Doubleday, a division of
Bantam Doubleday Dell Publishing Group, Inc.,
666 Fifth Avenue, New York, New York 10103

Doubleday and the portrayal of an anchor with a dolphin
are trademarks of Doubleday, a division of
Bantam Doubleday Dell Publishing Group, Inc.

Library of Congress Cataloging-in-Publication Data
O'Neill, Mary Le Duc, 1908–
Hailstones and halibut bones : adventures in color / by Mary
O'Neill ; newly illustrated by John Wallner.
p.   cm.
Summary: Twelve poems reflect the author's feelings about various
colors.
1. Color—Juvenile poetry.   2. Children's poetry, American,
[1. Color—Poetry.   2. American poetry.]   I. Wallner, John C., ill.
II. Title.
PS3565.N524H35   1989
811'.54—dc19   88-484
CIP
AC
ISBN 0-385-24484-3
ISBN 0-385-24485-1 (lib. bdg.)

Like acrobats on a high trapeze
The Colors pose and bend their knees
Twist and turn and leap and blend
Into shapes and feelings without end . . .

Introduction

I wrote this book almost by accident.

For many years off and on, I had been jotting down feelings about colors, the meanings of colors, wisps of ideas, fleeting impressions, all quite personal. They stayed in a desk drawer where I would come back to them when I had new thoughts and a little free time.

Then one winter I had a deadline. I'd been given an assignment and was getting nowhere with it. I remember the job—it was hard, it wasn't coming naturally, and it was due. My editor stopped by my home. She needed the piece. I had promised it, and it wasn't ready. In desperation, I thought, she asked if I had anything else she could use. I said no, but that she was welcome to leaf through the drawers of notes, poems, and never-finished stories.

After a while, she came back from my desk, suddenly excited, arms full of papers, eyes glowing. She had her piece, and she saw a book in those scraps and thoughts. The book was to become *Hailstones and Halibut Bones*.

I was surprised and flattered then, and continue to be, by the large audience—including the blind—who still write to me. I am very grateful to all these readers—the children in the United States, Canada, Australia, England, and Japan—who found the book simple as soup, and began to write their own compositions about color. I am also grateful to the university and college professors, librarians, and high school and grade school teachers who hailed it in its beginning and still use it in their classrooms, to the host of reviewers and writers who praised it, and to my publisher, Doubleday, for their decision to bring out this new edition for a new generation of readers.

What Is Purple?

Time is purple
Just before night
When most people
Turn on the light——
But if you don't it's
A beautiful sight.
Asters are purple,
There's purple ink.
Purple's more popular
Than you think. . . .
It's sort of a great
Grandmother to pink.
There are purple shadows
And purple veils,
Some ladies purple
Their fingernails.

There's purple jam
And purple jell
And a purple bruise
Next day will tell
Where you landed
When you fell.
The purple feeling
Is rather put-out
The purple look is a
Definite pout.
But the purple sound
Is the loveliest thing
It's a violet opening
In the spring.

What Is Gold?

Gold is a metal
Gold is a ring
Gold is a very
Beautiful thing.
Gold is the sunshine
Light and thin
Warm as a muffin
On your skin.
Gold is the moon
Gold are the stars;
Jupiter, Venus
Saturn and Mars,

Gold is the color of
Clover honey
Gold is a certain
Kind of money.
Gold is alive
In a flickering fish
That lives its life
In a crystal dish.
Gold is the answer
To many a wish.
Gold is feeling
Like a king
It's like having the most
Of everything——
Long time ago
I was told
Yellow's mother's name
Is gold. . . .

What Is Black?

Black is the night
When there isn't a star
And you can't tell by looking
Where you are.
Black is a pail of paving tar.
Black is jet
And things you'd like to forget.
Black is a smokestack
Black is a cat,
A leopard, a raven,
A high silk hat.
The sound of black is
"Boom! Boom! Boom!"
Echoing in
An empty room.

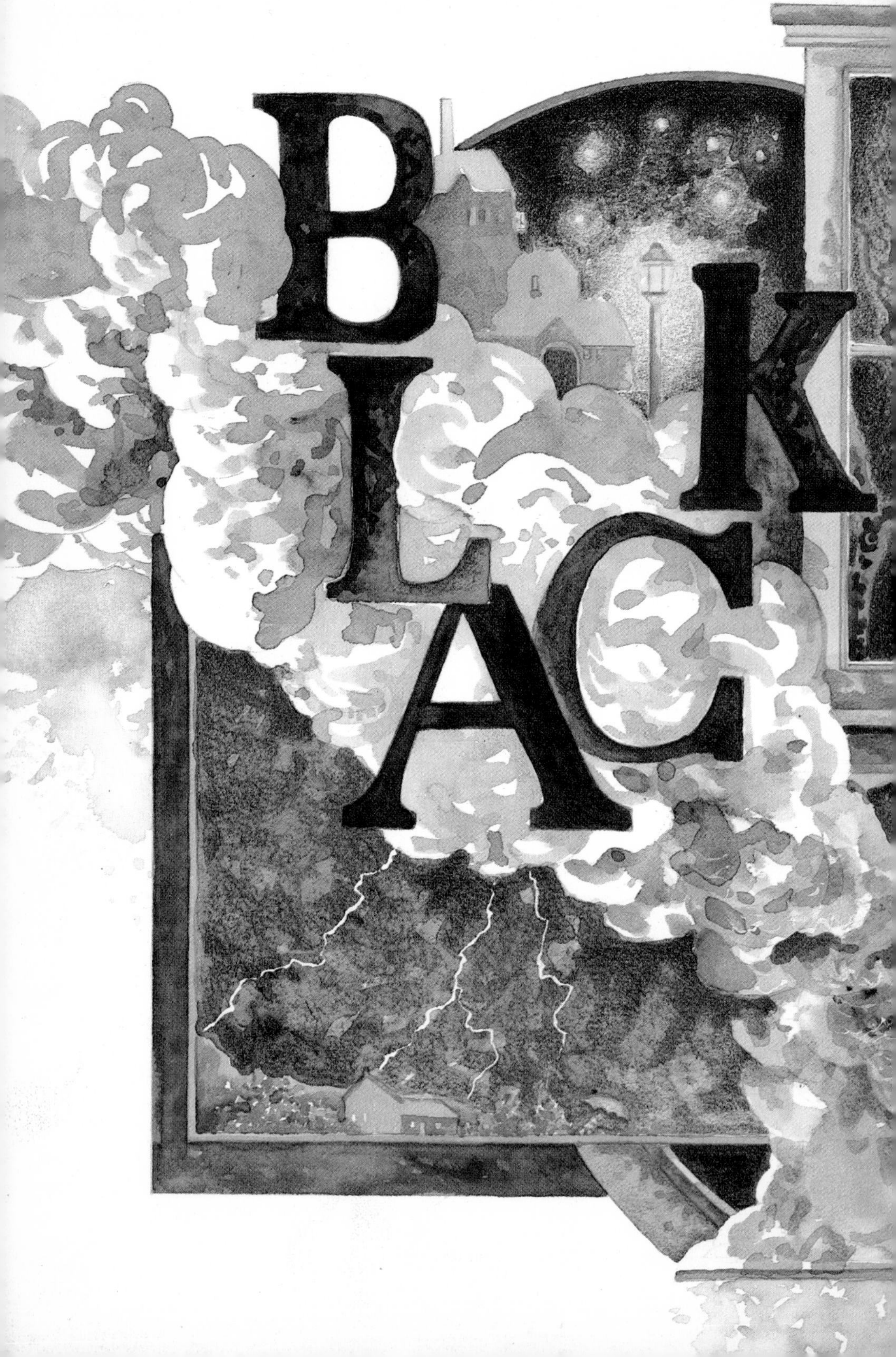
BLACK

Black is kind——
It covers up
The run-down street,
The broken cup.
Black is charcoal
And patio grill,
The soot spots on
The window sill.
Black is a feeling
Hard to explain
Like suffering but
Without the pain.
Black is licorice
And patent leather shoes
Black is the print
In the news.
Black is beauty
In its deepest form,
The darkest cloud
In a thunderstorm.
Think of what starlight
And lamplight would lack
Diamonds and fireflies
If they couldn't lean against
Black. . . .

What Is Brown?

Brown is the color of a country road
Back of a turtle
Back of a toad.
Brown is cinnamon
And morning toast
And the good smell of
The Sunday roast.
Brown is the color of work
And the sound of a river,
Brown is bronze and a bow
And a quiver.
Brown is the house
On the edge of town
Where wind is tearing
The shingles down.

Brown is a freckle
Brown is a mole
Brown is the earth
When you dig a hole.
Brown is the hair
On many a head
Brown is chocolate
And gingerbread.
Brown is a feeling
You get inside
When wondering makes
Your mind grow wide.
Brown is a leather shoe
And a good glove——
Brown is as comfortable
As love.

What Is Blue?

Blue is the color of the sky
Without a cloud
Cool, distant, beautiful
And proud.
Blue is the quiet sea
And the eyes of some people,
And many agree
As they grow older and older
Blue is the scarf
Spring wears on her shoulder.
Blue is twilight,
Shadows on snow,
Blue is feeling
Way down low.

Blue is a heron,
A sapphire ring,
You can smell blue
In many a thing:
Gentian and larkspur
Forget-me-nots, too.
And if you listen
You can hear blue
In wind over water
And wherever flax blooms
And when evening steps into
Lonely rooms.
Cold is blue:
Flame shot from a welding torch
Is, too:
Hot, wild, screaming, blistering Blue—
And on winter mornings
The dawns are blue. . . .

What Is Gray?

Gray is the color of an elephant
And a mouse
And a falling-apart house.
It's fog and smog,
Fine print and lint,
It's a hush and
The bubbling of oatmeal mush.
Tiredness and oysters
Both are gray,

Smoke swirls
And grandmother curls.
So are some spring coats
And nannygoats.
Eagles are gray
And a rainy day
The sad look of a slum
And chewing gum
Wood ash and linen crash.
Pussywillows are gray
In a velvety way.
Suits, shoes
And bad news,
Beggars' hats
And alley cats
Skin of a mole
And a worn slipper sole.
Content is gray
And sleepiness, too
They wear gray suede gloves
When they're touching you. . . .

What Is White?

White is a dove
And lily of the valley
And a puddle of milk
Spilled in an alley——
A ship's sail
A kite's tail
A wedding veil
Hailstones and
Halibut bones
And some people's
Telephones.
The hottest and most blinding light
Is white.
And breath is white
When you blow it out on a frosty night.
White is the shining absence of all color
Then absence is white
Out of touch
Out of sight.

White is marshmallow
And vanilla ice cream
And the part you can't remember
In a dream.
White is the sound
Of a light foot walking
White is a pair of
Whispers talking.
White is the beautiful
Broken lace
Of snowflakes falling
On your face.
You can smell white
In a country room
Toward the end of May
In the cherry bloom.

What Is Orange?

Orange is a tiger lily,
A carrot,
A feather from
A parrot,
A flame,
The wildest color
You can name.
Orange is a happy day
Saying good-by
In a sunset that
Shocks the sky.
Orange is brave
Orange is bold
It's bittersweet
And marigold.

Orange is zip
Orange is dash
The brightest stripe
In a Roman sash.
Orange is an orange
Also a mango
Orange is music
Of the tango.
Orange is the fur
Of the fiery fox,
The brightest crayon
In the box.
And in the fall
When the leaves are turning
Orange is the smell
Of a bonfire burning. . . .

What Is Red?

Red is a sunset
Blazy and bright.
Red is feeling brave
With all your might.
Red is a sunburn
Spot on your nose,
Sometimes red
Is a red, red rose.
Red squiggles out
When you cut your hand.
Red is a brick and
A rubber band.
Red is a hotness
You get inside
When you're embarrassed
And want to hide.

Fire-cracker, fire-engine
Fire-flicker red——
And when you're angry
Red runs through your head.
Red is an Indian,
A Valentine heart,
The trimming on
A circus cart.
Red is a lipstick,
Red is a shout,
Red is a signal
That says: "Watch out!"
Red is a great big
Rubber ball.
Red is the giant-est
Color of all.
Red is a show-off
No doubt about it——
But can you imagine
Living without it?

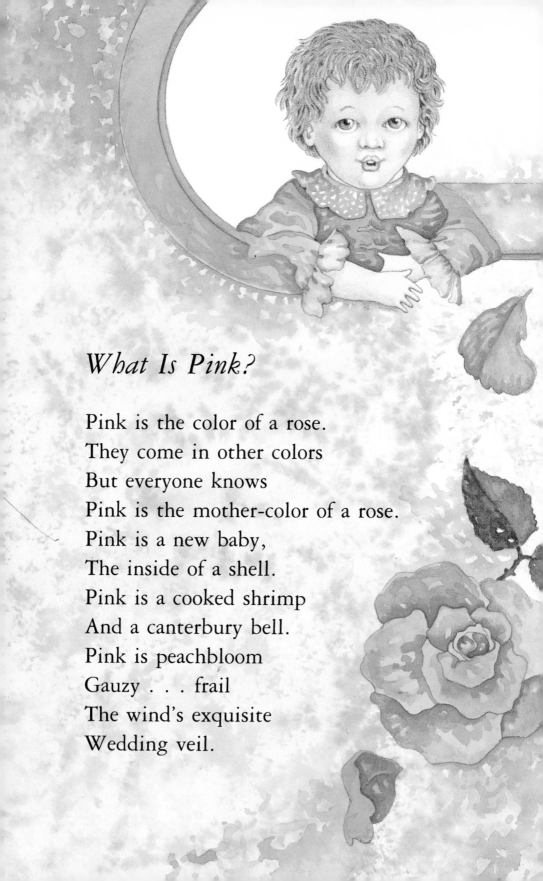

What Is Pink?

Pink is the color of a rose.
They come in other colors
But everyone knows
Pink is the mother-color of a rose.
Pink is a new baby,
The inside of a shell.
Pink is a cooked shrimp
And a canterbury bell.
Pink is peachbloom
Gauzy . . . frail
The wind's exquisite
Wedding veil.

Pink is a bonbon,
Pink is a blush,
Some Easter bunnies
Are pink plush.
If you stand in an orchard
In the middle of Spring
And you don't make a sound
You can hear pink sing,
A darling, whispery
Song of a thing.

Pink is the beautiful
Little sister of red
My teacher said,
And a ribbon girls tie
Round their head.
Pink is the sash
With the lovely fold
You'll remember
When you're old.
Pink is the flower
On a lady's hat
That nods and bows
This way and that.

What Is Green?

Green is the grass
And the leaves of trees
Green is the smell
Of a country breeze.
Green is lettuce
And sometimes the sea.
When green is a feeling
You pronounce it N.V.
Green is a coolness
You get in the shade
Of the tall old woods
Where the moss is made.

Green is a flutter
That comes in Spring
When frost melts out
Of everything.
Green is a grasshopper
Green is jade
Green is hiding
In the shade——
Green is an olive
And a pickle.
The sound of green
Is a water-trickle
Green is the world
After the rain
Bathed and beautiful
Again.

April is green
Peppermint, too.
Every elf has
One green shoe.
Under a grape arbor
Air is green
With sprinkles of sunlight
In between.
Green is the meadow,
Green is the fuzz
That covers up
Where winter was.
Green is ivy and
Honeysuckle vine.
Green is yours
Green is mine. . . .

What Is Yellow?

Yellow is the color of the sun
The feeling of fun
The yolk of an egg
A duck's bill
A canary bird
And a daffodil.
Yellow's sweet corn
Ripe oats
Hummingbirds'
Little throats
Summer squash and
Chinese silk
The cream on top
Of Jersey milk
Dandelions and
Daisy hearts
Custard pies and
Lemon tarts.

Yellow blinks
On summer nights
In the off-and-on of
Firefly lights.
Yellow's a topaz
A candle flame.
Felicity's a
Yellow name.
Yellow's mimosa,
And I guess,
Yellow's the color of
Happiness.

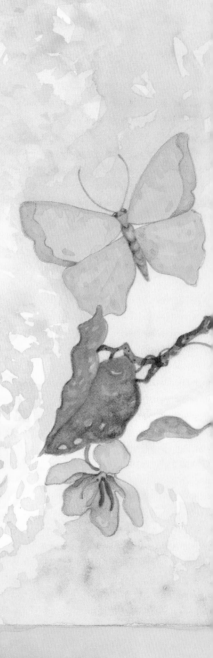

The Colors live
Between black and white
In a land that we
Know best by sight.
But knowing best
Isn't everything,
For colors dance
And colors sing,

And colors laugh
And colors cry———
Turn off the light
And colors die,
And they make you feel
Every feeling there is
From the grumpiest grump
To the fizziest fizz.
And you and you and I
Know well
Each has a taste
And each has a smell
And each has a wonderful
Story to tell. . . .

About the Author

Mary O'Neill was raised in what she describes as a wonderful barn of a Victorian house in Berea, Ohio, where she wrote and directed plays for her younger brothers and sisters. She decided quite early that she wanted to write for a living, but her writing had to be confined to spare-time recreation.

She entered the advertising field as a copywriter for a department store, and one by one, the stories written for recreation began to be accepted by leading national magazines, including *McCall's, Woman's Day, Ladies' Home Journal, Reader's Digest, Parents' Magazine, Scholastic,* and others.

After becoming a partner in her own advertising agency, Mrs. O'Neill moved to New York, spending her time as author and housewife.

Though she has written several books for Doubleday, *Hailstones and Halibut Bones* is without a doubt the author's most renowned work; since its original publication in 1961, it has become a modern classic.

It has gone through more than thirty printings, been published in several countries and languages, including Braille, and has been praised by both readers and educators around the world.

Mrs. O'Neill, the mother of three grown children, is now living in Arizona.

About the Artist

John C. Wallner is the award-winning illustrator of more than thirty books for children. His many awards and honors include several American Library Association Notable Books of the Year, the Certificate of Excellence from the American Institute of Graphic Arts (1980), the Friends of American Writers Award for Best Illustrator (1977), and five Certificates of Merit from the Society of Illustrators. In addition, he has been critically acclaimed by book reviewers. One of his most recent titles contains "lush, provocative paintings" according to *School Library* Journal, while *Publishers Weekly* called it a "beautiful book."

He holds a master's degree in Fine Arts from Pratt Institute and currently resides in upstate New York with his wife, who is also an artist.